JOY OF LIVING

Cacti and Other Succulents

Manufactured in the United States of America
1 2 3 4 5 6 7 8 9 10

Library of Congress Cataloging in Publication Data

Main entry under title:

Cacti and other succulents.

1. Cactus. 2. Succulent plants.
I. Consumer guide
SB438.C27 635.9'33'47 76-18259
ISBN 0-671-22412-3
Trade distribution by Simon and Schuster
A Gulf + Western Company
Rockefeller Center, 630 Fifth Avenue
New York, New York 10020

JOY OF LIVING

Cacti and Other Succulents

A complete guide to cacti and other succulents of great character and beauty. All you need to know about care and maintenance, potting and propagation.

Cover designer: Frank E. Peiler
Horticultural consultant: Virginia L. Beatty
Illustrator: Clarence Moberg
Photographer: William Miller
Plants: Courtesy of Erickson's Tropical and Green Plants (Addison, IL); Ted's Greenhouse (Tinley Park, IL): Tropical Plants Rentals, Inc. (Prairie View, IL)

Introduction

Almost everyone knows that a cactus can go a long time between drinks, but there are a number of plants in other families — crassula, euphorbia and lily — that can do the same thing. Succulents are plants of great character and, some people think, of great beauty. They often have thick, fleshy leaves that store water, and are engineered in such a way that they expose the least amount of surface to the sun and winds. The stems are usually thick and filled with water-storing tissue. Some succulents have lost all their leaves or lose their leaves regularly when things get bad. The work usually done by the leaves is then carried on by the stem. In some succulents the stem is compact and has ridges like an accordion that expand and contract with the water supply. In competing for survival in arid areas, many succulents have evolved sharp spines to protect themselves from predators. Some plants from the most arid areas have many spines that also serve to shade the plant. Living under the same stressful conditions has caused plants from very different families to look superficially quite the same. For example, the corn cob cactus is really a ***Euphorbia mammillaris.***

Cacti from desert areas, like the ***Mammillaria*** and ***Echinocactus,*** are plump and spiny while those that originally grew in jungle areas are flat or thin and spineless like the ***Rhipsalis*** and ***Schlumbergera.*** There are even cacti with leaves. For instance, the ***Pereskia*** when full grown, looks a bit like an orange or grapefruit tree. Other succulents come from a number of families.The agave, milkweed, lily and crassula have many members. These plants, with or without spines, all have compact growth habits and lots of character.

Succulents are ideal plants for busy people since they need less humidity and water than most indoor plants. They are very tolerant of variations in temperature. They are interesting without flowers, but with flowers they are spectacular.

Since the advent of central heating succulents have been grown as indoor plants. They can tolerate the low humidity found indoors in winter.

Succulents are an investment: the longer they grow the more magnificent they become.

Care and Maintenance

Some people grow succulents just like their other plants, keeping them warm, watered and well fed. If the drainage is excellent the plants will flourish, get pleasingly plump (some cacti may even grow leaves) and lose the stark bony beauty that caused people to fall in love with them in the first place.

Light

The succulents that do have spines need bright light to grow well but they will exist with less. Confined in pots next to a window they may sunburn. Protect them from concentrated rays of the sun. Succulents without spines do well in bright to filtered light with protection from very hot sun.

Light and Day Length

Cacti and other succulents do well in 16 hours of fluorescent light mixed with incandescent light in a ratio of 10 watts of fluorescent to one watt of incandescent light. If you want flowers, you will have to do a little studying on your plants' individual requirements. Some need to be kept cool for a while and others need a good rest with plenty of darkness before they will flower. Christmas cactus, ***Schlumbergera bridgesii,*** for example, should be kept rather dry — below 60°F and given eight hour days (16 hour nights) to encourage blooming. Set your timer or cover the plant each night with an opaque, black cloth.

In the plant description the words are defined as follows:

Bright. This means bright light or full sun with no curtains or blinds between the plant and the window. On the other side of the window, there is no tree, sign or building to obstruct the light from the outside. In bright light, when you hold your hand a foot over a sheet of paper, you get a clear, sharp shadow.

Filtered. This means sunlight which is diffused by a glass curtain in the window. In filtered light, your hand makes a fuzzy, but distinguishable shadow when held a foot above a sheet of typing paper.

Shady. This means no direct sun or other light, and your hand held a foot over a sheet of paper will produce nothing more than a blob. All plants that tolerate shade need high humidity.

Water and Humidity

Do a thorough job when watering cacti and other succulents. Think of a cloudburst in the desert. Then let them go a long time until the next drink. In the winter, many cacti become dormant and watering should be restricted. African succulents often go into dormancy in the summertime; when they are in this state, hold back on the water. Water combined with cold or dormancy spells disaster.

When the plants are actively growing, water them quite frequently and keep them moderately moist. Water and warmth while the plants are growing spells growth.

Cacti and other succulents can tolerate the dry air very well, even though the air in most houses and apartments in winter is drier than that in the deserts.

In the plant descriptions, the general watering suggestions are given as follows:

Drench and Let Dry. Soak the plant thoroughly by submerging the pot in a bucket or sink filled with tepid water. Wait until all the bubbles have stopped coming out. The plant can then dry until its next soaking, which should take place when the surface of the soil is dry to the touch. Most of the plants that prefer drenching and drying have thick roots.

Moist. Keep the soil evenly moist but never soggy or too dry.

Wet. Keep the soil wet at all times.

Temperature and Air Circulation

As long as they are dry, most succulents are very tolerant. They can take temperatures from 45°F to 85°F without complaint as long as they are dry. There are even cacti that survive outside all year long in Canada and Alaska. Succulents don't care for stuffy environments, especially when they are wet. Keep plants well separated and give them plenty of air. Night temperatures below 65°F and less than 12 hours of light are required to encourage most succulents into bloom.

Most plants prefer a distinct difference between their night and day temperatures; with the night temperature being more important to a plant's growth.

In the plant descriptions, the general temperature and air suggestions are given as follows:

Cold. Night temperatures of 40° to 45°F.

Cool. Night temperatures of 50° to 55°F. A good many of the old-fashioned favorites are in this category. When these plants look listless and not quite bright, they probably had a bad night.

House. Night temperatures of 60° to 65°F. These are what used to be called stovehouse or hothouse plants.

Dry. The typical modern house, apartment or office contains half the percentage of moisture that's found in the Sahara.

Circulating. Plants which need fresh air and good ventilation.

Fertilizer

Old and well established plants that are actively growing can benefit occasionally from a dilute liquid fertilizer. Succulents are accustomed to having it tough. If you aren't sure they can use help, don't fertilize. If you are growing your succulents warm and wet, they will need more fertilizer, but use restraint.

Pests and Diseases

After people, the most frequent pests are mealybugs, nematodes and scale. If you get nematodes, remove all the soil from the roots and repot using pasteurized soil or mix. For mealybugs and scale, depending on the number of spines the plant has, a good scrub with an old toothbrush and warm soapy water can do wonders. If you are using chemical sprays, read the label very carefully since some popular sprays, such as malathion, can injure succulents as much as the pest.

The most serious diseases are rots. Rots can be aggravated by improper watering, forcing growth during periods of dormancy and wounding plants when repotting. Sometimes the plant can be saved by cutting out and removing material one-half inch beyond the area that looks decayed. The wound should be washed with a solution of one part household bleach and nine parts water. The plant should be kept in intensive care in an area of low humidity until it recovers. Unless it is special, get rid of it.

General Maintenance

These plants have been self-sufficient for centuries, and if left to themselves and given good light, they will do very well. Keep them clean; give the pots plenty of room. Watch for the occasional pest. Most care is on the negative side. Don't fuss, don't overwater, don't over-feed — let the plants do their thing.

Potting and Repotting

Cacti and other succulents can be kept in a dish garden when small. The clay trays often used for bonsai are very good for a start. When the plants get too big they can be transplanted into their own pots. If you keep the plants dry they will stay the same size whether the temperature is 45°F or 85°F. If you water the plants when the temperature is low or while they are dormant they will rot.

Don't overpot. Overpotting often leads to rotting of roots. If the plant is top heavy, put the smaller pot inside a larger pot and fill the space between the two with gravel. This will give the plant a heavy enough base without running the risk of rot.

Pot Size

Pot cacti and other succulents in containers that are as small as possible. For cacti, use a pot just large enough to fit the plant. For other succulents, use a pot just slightly larger than the root ball.

For some plants, the holes in the bottom of the pot do not provide enough drainage. Use a hammer and a screwdriver to make the hole larger in a clay pot. Use a hot knife or a hot ice pick for a plastic pot. In either case, be careful not to break the pot or burn yourself. If you do break the clay pot, don't throw it away — you can use the pieces for your next planting project.

Soil

Excellent drainage is more important than the potting material. The soil should be porous and should be spread over a deep layer of gravel or broken bricks. The spineless succulents appreciate more humus (organic matter) in their potting mix.

In the plant descriptions the general soil suggestions are given as follows:

Heavy. This is made of good garden soil, clay or loam with about one-third humus. When good drainage is required, it should contain about one-third washed builder's sand or perlite.

Organic. This is soil rich in humus, leaf mold (disintegrated leaves) or some other organic material. Coarse builder's sand or perlite will improve the drainage.

Light. This means open-textured material with excellent drainage that can be kept moist but never wet. It is good for plants that in nature spend their time in trees.

How to Pot

1. Select a pot that is not too large.
2. Put sufficient drainage material

in the bottom.
3. Fill it about one-third full with your potting material.
4. Test the plant for size (make sure that the plant won't be too far down in the pot nor too high above the top of the pot). Center the plant unless it's the kind that likes to travel in a horizontal direction, in which case it should be put at one edge.
5. Now, gently holding the plant where you would like it to stay, fill all the spaces between the plant and the pot with your potting medium.
6. Press the soil gently down around the roots and shake the pot so the soil will settle. If there isn't enough soil or if the soil packs down, add some more. You pack the soil more tightly around old plants than around seedlings. Leave space between the top of the medium and the top of the pot so you will have room for water.

Potting

7. Water the plant.

Repotting

With a plant that is already in a pot, the procedure is pretty much the same except that you have to start by removing the plant from pot number one. Sometimes the plant will slip out easily; but other times it's more of a problem. If the plant will not come out of the pot easily, do not yank on it. It may be better to break the container than to bruise the plant or break off its top.

How to Knock Out a Plant

If the plant is stuck in its pot, first tap the pot gently on a hard surface such as wood or concrete, and see if you can wriggle the plant out. If that doesn't work, take a knife and gently slip it around the inside of the pot to see if the plant will now come out. If that doesn't work, and the pot is clay, take your hammer and give the pot several sharp, controlled blows to break the pot without damaging the plant. If the pot is plastic, use a sharp knife to cut away the pot.

When the plant is out of the pot, remove some of the soil around the root ball. If the roots look overgrown, prune some of them away. In some plants where the roots get very, very thick, you can take a knife and just cut off the outside of the root ball including the roots. This root pruning can also be used if you want to keep your plant in the same size pot. By pruning away some of the roots and then taking off some of the top you can keep your plant "growing on" in the same pot for years.

How to Handle Spiny Plants

Use a newspaper folded into a narrow band to handle spiny plants. Wrap the band around the plant like a belt or harness. Use a fresh band for every plant. Gloves are not satisfactory since the large spines stab right through and the small spines break off in the glove, making the gloves uncomfortable to handle.

Propagation

Cacti and other succulents are easy to propagate. Any encouragement you can give them will start new growth. Remember that they are accustomed to growing on the dry side and too much water or humidity will cause them to rot.

For successful propagation of any kind you will need to:

- Develop mechanical and technical skills. Train the hand and eye. Many times the head will know how, but the hand can't do it. Skills improve with practice, and fortunately these plants are quite tolerant.
- Know the plants' structures and how they grow. You can learn this by working with plants — let them teach you — or you can read, take formal courses, or a combination of these. If you understand how plants grow, you will have an easier time propagating them and be better able to cope with the unexpected.
- Know the different kinds of plants and the methods by which they can be propagated. The form of propagation used depends on the plant and your circumstances.

Division

Division is the easiest form of multiplication. It is not only easy on you but also on the plant. Division is ideal when you want only a few plants, or you can use it when the plant starts crowding in on itself. Division is not an extreme form of reproduction. Done gently, it's an operation that is only slightly more traumatic than transplanting. There is trauma, since the root ball is being separated and a part rather than the whole plant is being potted up; but you have roots, stem and leaves (if not the leaves, at least the shoots to produce them). All you need to do is encourage each part to keep on growing and protect it

Division

until it gets over the effects of the separation. Some plants divide easily while others require the eye of a diamond cutter to make the most of the possibilities.

Division of indoor plants can take place at any time, but it is especially successful from the plant's point of view if done during the winter when the plant is resting — indoor gardeners are less busy then, too. Dividing plants in the winter is frustrating from the indoor gardener's point of view because the plants will just sit there and do nothing until it is time for them to come out of their dormancy and start growing with enthusiasm.

Many succulents, especially those with thick mats of sprawling growth, can be divided very easily. They do very well, particularly if the division takes place at the beginning of their growing season.

What You Will Need

Before beginning to divide a plant, collect everything you will need:

- The plant to be operated on.
- Newspapers.
- Bucket of warm water.
- Clean pots.
- Fresh, clean soil.
- Drainage aids.
- Sterile knife.
- Plenty of time.

How to Divide Plants

1. Spread the newspapers out carefully. Often the hardest part of dividing a plant is cleaning up the mess afterwards.
2. Remove the plant from its pot. Do this gently: break the pot if necessary.
3. Decide how many plants the division is to produce.
4. Separate the root ball gently. If the roots are damaged or torn off, you will have a large cutting rather than a plant division and growth will be slowed. At times, a clean sharp knife or a hatchet is necessary to divide the root ball with the least amount of bruising. A clean cut is better than a torn and mangled mess caused by pulling and yanking. If you are not sure how the plant is structured under the soil line, put the root ball into a bucket of warm water and gently tease the parts of the plant apart. There will be some damage to some of the roots, but you will be able to see where the main divisions are. If you are gentle and repot carefully this can be a useful method, especially when working with plants that have become extremely rootbound.
5. Be sure that each division has roots, stem and leaves (or shoots), and pot it in a clean, proper-sized pot with good drainage. Good drainage is very important because the roots have been disturbed and damaged roots are more susceptible to rot.
6. Use fresh, sterile, or at least uninhabited soil. Unless there is a good reason for doing otherwise, place the division in the center of the pot.
7. Plant each division as deep as it was growing before. Press the soil firmly around the plant and water with warm water. Roll up all the debris in the newspaper and clean the operating area. Put the separated plants in a protected location (out of full sun and drafts) for a few days. In a relatively short time the plants will have adjusted themselves to their new conditions and they will be full-fledged members of your col-

lection or ready to join someone else's indoor garden.

Cuttings

Most succulents root easily from a piece of the plant or from leaves. It is important to let the piece dry out a bit before planting. Fleshy leaves taken off of succulents can be put where they are warm and dry and they will start sending out roots. That is the time to pot them up. High humidity is not necessary and possibly harmful, but bottom heat is a big help.

In propagating plants by cuttings, a piece of root, stem or leaf is taken from the plant, kept under favorable conditions and encouraged to grow. This produces a new plant which is usually, but not always, identical to the original (a variegated ***Sansevieria*** cutting will grow plain green). For plants that can be easily propagated this way, there are a number of advantages. It is inexpensive, relatively fast and doesn't require a lot of know-how except on the part of the plant. Home is not always the ideal place to propagate plants, but with some plants the percentage of success is so great that one keeps wanting to start more.

For succulent leaf cuttings such as hens and chickens, burro tails, etc., choose mature leaves that are not in the process of dying. If you remove them with a sideways pull there is less chance of damage to the plant and a better chance that there will be a tiny piece of stem attached (having a bit of stem attached often means that you will get a new plant and not just a well-rooted leaf). Once the leaf has been removed, you can lay it on some potting soil or mix, or put it in a

Removing leaf

From leaf to plant

Stages in propagating succulents

cardboard box on top of the refrigerator or any other convenient place. In either case, don't water until the roots appear. After the roots and young plant start showing, the mix can be kept moist. (Pot up the ones you had in the box over the refrigerator when the roots and new plant appear.) The leaves may rot if you water them before this. When the new plantlets start growing, put them in a brighter light.

For ***Sansevieria*** cuttings, take a leaf, cut it into sections three to four inches long. Mark the top of each section by cutting a small notch out of the top. Plant the notch side up.

From Seed

Starting plants from seeds can be especially gratifying. The greatest satisfaction comes from growing plants from seed you have hybridized yourself. Each seed is a combination of the heredity characteristics of its parents. For this reason plants grown from seeds can vary tremendously. Many succulents grow very easily from seed if the seed is fresh, but they may take a long time to germinate. Also, succulents being very cautious plants may germinate only a few seeds at a time. Some seeds start germinating in two days and others may take two years. Seeds vary considerably in terms of their longevity and viability; many may not have enough vitality to survive beyond germination.

Start seeds in a well drained, sterile mix. Water sparingly but do not allow the seedlings to dry out. Seeds can not germinate until moisture has penetrated the hard seed coat. The taking up of moisture and swelling is a physical thing that may happen even with dead seed.

Because of the problems of seeds dying in the soil or seedlings dying just after they germinate, it is

New plants from old leaves

Stages in propagating cacti from seeds

usually best to start seedlings in an artificial mix.

Grafting

Grafting is used:

- To speed up the propagation of known varieties.
- To provide plants with a stronger root system. Many attractive plants grow faster or do not rot as easily if they are grown on plain but sturdy roots.
- To maintain "sports" or monsters that would not be able to survive on their own, such as a brightly colored cactus that contains no chlorophyll and is unable to feed itself.

Grafting can also be used to produce a shape or effect that would

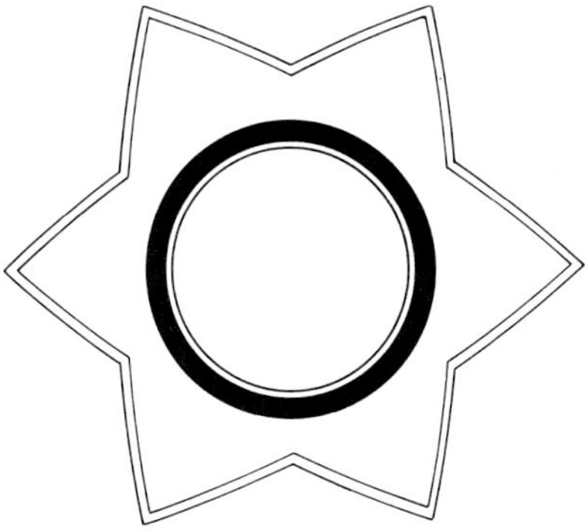

Vascular rings, same size

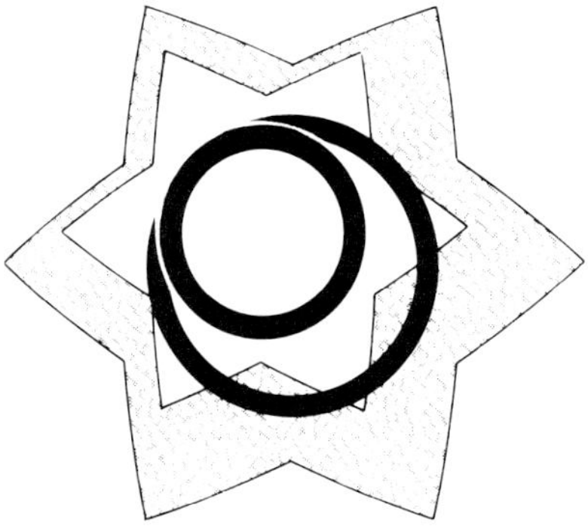

Slightly smaller

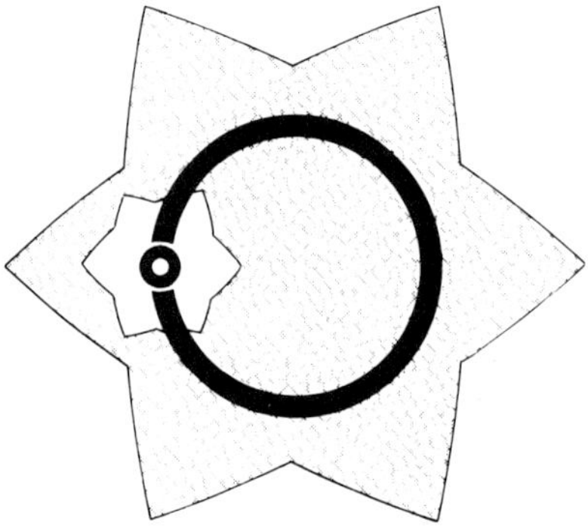

Much smaller

not have been possible with one plant alone. Dwarfed plants can be produced by using a dwarfing root stock or by inserting a dwarfing section in a stem. Weeping, tree-like effects can be produced by grafting vining or sprawling plants on top of a tall, upright base.

The principles are simple but success takes a keen eye, a steady hand and lots of practice. Failure is reduced by working quickly and keeping the plant parts, tools (knives or razor blades) and hands as aseptic (clean) as possible.

Grafting is done with compatible plants. Compatability generally, but not always, means plants in the same species, genus or family — plants that are somewhat similar in structure. Since the plants are the final judge of compatibility, grafting is very often a trial and error process — with the possibilities of some exciting surprises. If the diameter of one piece to be grafted is larger than the other, you will have to move the two pieces around so that as many of their actively growing cells as possible are in contact. The easiest graft to make is a flat graft where both the stock (the part with the roots) and the scion (the part to be added) are the same size and their vascular bundles (tubes that provide support and conduct water and nutrients) match. The drawings on this page show how the vascular bundles should be matched up when areas are of unequal size. A cleft or wedge graft is used when the scion is very narrow or flat. A one inch slit or wedge is cut into the top of the stock and the scion is trimmed on both sides are is inserted into the split. A side graft is sometimes used. In a side graft a slanting or diagonal cut is made on both the

Stages in grafting cacti

stock and scion. This cut often produces more surface area and a better chance for the graft to take.

When grafting cacti and other succulents, light weight rubber bands can be used to keep the pieces together or large spines can be used to pin them on.

Grafting is more successful when the plants are in their active growing period — usually in the spring through the fall. It is important that the stock plant is in good health and not neglected while the graft is taking. After grafting keep the plants in a shaded spot for a while to keep the cuts from drying too quickly. Keep water off the cuts to help guard against disease. Keep the contact firm between the stock and scion and do not remove the rubber bands or spines until a month after the graft appears to have taken.

In grafting, practice makes perfect. For greater success, as well as better looking results, keep your plants, tools and fingers hospital clean.

Sources

For Plants

Abbey Garden
Box 30331
Santa Barbara, CA 93105
Illustrated catalog.

Beahm Gardens
2686 Paloma St.
Pasadena, CA 91107
Catalog $.10.

Cox's Epiphyllum Nursery
90 McNeill
Encinitas, CA 92024
Illustrated catalog $.35

Davis Cactus Garden
1522 Jefferson St.
Kerville, TX 78028
Illustrated catalog $.25

Desert Dan's Cactus
W. Summer St.
Minotola, NJ 08341
Illustrated color catalog $.50

A. Hugh Dial
7585 Deer Trail
Yucca Valley, CA 92284
Price list

Grigsby Cactus Gardens
2326 Bella Vista Ave.
Vista, CA 92083
Illustrated catalog $.50 (credited)

Ben Haines Co.
1902 Lane
Topeka, KS 66604
Price list

Hawks Epiphyllum Nursery
11918 E. Lambert
El Monte, CA 91732
Catalog $.35 (credited)

Henrietta's Nursery
12712 Stockton Blvd.
Galt, CA 95632
Illustrated catalog $.50 (credited)

McPherson Gardens
2920 Starr Ave.
Oregon, OH 43616
Illustrated catalog

New Mexico Cactus Research
Box 787
Belen, NM 87702
Price list

Oakhill Gardens
Rt. 3, Box 87m
Dallas, OR 97338
Catalog.

For Information

Cactus and Succulent Society of America
1593 Las Canos Rd.
Santa Barbara, CA 93105
Journal, bimonthly.
Annual dues $10.00

Epiphyllum Society of America
218 E. Greystone Ave.
Monrovia, CA 91016
Bulletin, six or more times a year.
Annual dues $3.00,
Gene Luckenbacher, Secretary
4400 Portola Ave.
Los Angeles, CA 90032

International Cactus and Succulent Society
Box 1452
San Angelo, TX 76901
Newsletter, three or more times a year. Annual dues $5.00

The Sempervivum Society
11 Wingle Tye Rd.
Burgess Hill, Sussex, England.
Journal, quarterly.
Annual dues $4.50.

Plant Names

Plants are listed alphabetically by their scientific names. The scientific name identifies the plant exactly since there are often many plants with the same, or similar, common name. In the plant descriptions, some of the common names are given in parentheses following the scientific names.

Plant Descriptions

AEONIUM

The ***Aeoniums*** are native to the Canary Islands and the Mediterranean region of North Africa. If a plant looks like a hens and chickens on top of a thick stalk it is possibly an aeonium. They look very much like the sempervivums of Europe and the echeverias of Mexico and Central America. Aeonium flowers, which are usually yellow, come out of the growing points in the center of the rosette. In most cases the plant dies after flowering when the seed matures. Don't be too hasty in composting the plant, though, new rosettes sometimes appear lower down on the stems. Most aeoniums are easy to grow if they get bright light in the winter, filtered light in summer, cool nights and good air circulation. They should be drenched and let dry between waterings, but make sure you have given them excellent drainage. While they are dormant or cold (they can take temperatures to 45°F) they need less water. When dormant, aeoniums often drop their leaves—if your aeonium has not flowered it is probably just resting. ***Aeonium arboreum*** (saucer plant) grows up to three feet tall and has rosettes six to eight inches across. The color commonly is green, but there are varieties striped with cream and some that are reddish or purple. The purple variety, ***Aeonium arboreum 'Schwartzkopf',*** needs much stronger light to keep

Aeonium arboreum 'Schwartzkopf'

Aeonium

Aeonium decorum cristatum

its dark purple color. ***Aeonium canariense*** (giant velvet rose) has large, floppy, green velvet rosettes. In ***Aeonium decorum cristatum*** the succulent stem is flattened at the top like a fan and covered along the top edge with rosettes of small leaves. ***Aeonium pseudotabulaeforme*** and ***Aeonium tabulaeforme*** both have flat platelike rosettes, except that the "pseudo" one is not quite as precise and tablelike. Aeoniums can be reproduced from seeds and leaf cuttings. Indoors, they may never set seed. If you plan to make leaf cuttings, do it while the plants are young and vigorous. Do not wait until they are in their final decline. At that time the leaves may not have enough vitality to root.

AGAVE

The ***Agave*** are the American look-a-like of the African ***Aloe.*** Both have heavy, stiff leaves formed into basal rosettes and tall spikes of flowers. The greatest difference between them is in their way of flowering. The flower stalks of the agaves develop from the growing point and those of the aloes grow from between the leaves. Thus, the agaves die after flowering while the aloes do not. Agaves are important in the production of fiber for rope and string. The sap is used in producing pulque, a beerlike drink (6 percent alcohol) and tequila, a distilled liquor (40 to 50 percent alcohol). ***Agave americana*** (century plant) originated in Mexico. The fleshy, grey-green leaves in the rosette can sometimes grow four feet long indoors. Each rosette leaf ends in a sharp, needlelike spine. These

Aeonium arboreum

Agave americana

Agave americana 'Marginata'

Agave leopoldii

natural needles, with the attached fiber, are used in Mexico to sew up heavy sacks. The century plant will grow many years before blooming when kept confined in a pot. There are several varieties of ***Agave americana***. ***Agave americana 'Marginata'*** has a creamy-yellow stripe on the edge of the leaf. ***Agave americana 'Medio-picta'*** has yellowish stripes down the center. ***Agave leopoldii*** is one of the smaller, slower growing agaves. Its dense rosette is made up of light green leaves that have white stripes on the sides and fibers on the edges that curl up like fine shavings. ***Agave victoriae-reginae*** is a compact rosette of thick, dark green leaves. The leaves are triangular in cross-section, have smooth, white edges and a blunt, dark spine at the end. This is a very slow growing plant.

Agaves prefer bright light but will tolerate less. Almost any soil will do if the drainage is excellent. They prefer cool nights but will tolerate house temperatures and dry air.

ALLUAUDIA
procera

Alluaudia procera, from southwest Madagascar, looks a lot like a crown of thorns, except that the leaves, when it has them, often grow much larger. The plant can grow rather tall—six feet high indoors and thirty-six feet tall in its native haunts. The stems are covered with sharp, tapering thorns or spines. When leaves do appear, they are oval and two or more inches long. Give it bright light, heavy soil with plenty of drainage, circulating air and cool or house

Agave victoriae-reginae

Alluaudia procera

Aloe arborescens

temperatures. Drench and let dry. It will often drop all its leaves when it decides to take a rest. When this happens, cut down on the watering until the leaves start to appear again. This is an interesting succulent and one that is not seen in every collection.

Aloe vera

ALOE

The ***Aloe*** somewhat resemble the ***Agaves*** but they grow faster and have different kinds of flowers. Most importantly, they do not die after blooming since the flower stalk grows out from between the leaves rather than from the central growing point. The tubelike flowers range in color from yellow to red. ***Aloe arborescens*** (candelabra aloe) is a succulent plant with tapering, blue-green leaves that grow up to two feet long. The leaves have teeth along the edges, but they are not as strong as those of the agave. As the plant grows older, it gets a number of branches. This is an interesting plant with strong definite lines and red flowers that appear around the first of the year. ***Aloe variegata*** (partridge breast, tiger

Aloe vera

aloe) has white-spotted, blue-green leaves that can grow ten inches long. The leaves have warty, saw-toothed edges, are triangular in cross section and are arranged in three neat stacks or ranks. ***Aloe vera*** (medicine plant, burn plant, lily of the desert) is a succulent plant with grey-green leaves that can grow over a foot long. The watery-looking, irregularly splotched leaves have feeble, fleshy spines along their edges. It occasionally has yellow flowers. The squashed leaves can be used to relieve burns, chapping and other skin irritations.

Bright light is necessary for aloes to flower, but they will survive in less light. They like dry air and cool night temperatures (50° to 55°F). Drench and let dry. During the wintertime, aloes need much less water than during the summertime, and they will tolerate temperatures just barely above freezing. Generally, they are very accommodating plants and live happily in house temperatures all year round if they have good drainage and are not killed off with excessive water.

APOROCACTUS flagelliformis

Aporocactus flagelliformis (rat tail cactus, rat's tail cactus) has thin weak stems (usually about a half inch in diameter) that can grow five feet long and hang down over the sides of its pot. The stems are covered with short, reddish brown spines. The two to three inch long red flowers can last for several days. The rat tail cactus needs bright light and coarse heavy soil with excellent drainage. Drench and let dry, but water more sparingly during the winter. Air that is too dry can encourage red spider; air that is too moist can encourage rot. In winter keep the plants cold and dry to encourage blooming. In Mexico they grow at high altitudes where the night temperatures are very brisk. In rural areas the dried flowers are used medicinally. They are often planted in the open end of a cow's horn, making an interesting decoration. This is an old-timer which is probably more often acquired as a cutting from a friend than through purchase.

ASPARAGUS meyeri

Asparagus meyeri (foxtail asparagus fern) has stems up to two feet long. Although it looks like a fern, it is a member of the lily family and originally came from South Africa. Its thick white roots help it survive in unfriendly environments. If it gets too dry or too warm its

Asparagus meyeri

Aporocactus flagelliformis

leaves turn yellow and drop. The foxtail asparagus looks its best when it is given filtered light, evenly moist heavy soil and a cool night temperature with good air circulation. Since the roots make such a heavy mat that the water will run off the top, occasionally soak the whole pot in a bucket of water.

BEAUCARNEA recurvata

Beaucarnea recurvata (bottle palm, elephant foot, pony tail) is a fascinating accent plant that will, in time, develop a trunk six to eight feet tall. It will then have a swollen base and a rosette of long, thin, straplike leaves (often growing down lower than the top of the pot). It prefers heavy soil, bright light, good drainage and should be allowed to dry out between waterings. This plant is ideal for people who travel a lot since it can last a long time on the water it stores in its trunk. An excellent indoor plant, it keeps its shape without having to be pinched, pruned or prodded. Because the leaves will sometimes grow very long and curled, it is shown to advantage in a hanging container or raised up on a pedestal.

Beaucarnea recurvata

Calibanus hookerii

CALIBANUS hookerii

Calibanus hookerii, from Mexico, is an interesting looking plant that is related to the agaves. It has tuberous roots and grasslike leaves. A very tolerant plant, it prefers bright light but will take less. It needs heavy soil with excellent drainage and circulating dry air. It is a tough plant. Having been bred to endure dry air and drought, it will survive for years in less than ideal conditions. However, it cannot cope too well with humid air, overwatering and too much fertilizer. It can stay in the same pot for a number of years since it prefers to be a bit rootbound. To keep it in shape, give it benign neglect.

Variety of forms for Cereus peruvianus

CEREUS peruvianus

Cereus peruvianus (torch cactus, hedge cactus, torch thistle) is a columnar cactus that can grow very large. Despite its name, it did not come from Peru; it probably originated someplace in central Brazil. Once upon a time it was the largest cactus group, but now it includes only the columnar tree cactus. It is widely cultivated in tropical America and often grows fifteen to twenty feet tall. It is the stereotype cactus for all the south-of-the-border cartoons. When mature, it develops heavy branches. Indoors, it can grow quite large; there is sometimes a problem keeping it upright when it gets top-heavy. The stems have five to eight flat ribs that often have clusters of brown spines along the outside edge. It makes an excellent hedge that is better at containing cattle than barbed wire. The mature plants have large, white flowers and bloom quite profusely.

Give it bright light, heavy soil with good drainage and house temperatures. Drench and let dry, but be careful not to overwater in the winter time or it will rot. Give it a bath every so often to free it of dust and grime. It grows very

Variety from single fruit of Cereus

Ceropegia woodii

easily from seed and will produce a great variety of forms—lumpy, bumpy and monstrous—from a single fruit. You can tell if a plant has been grown from a seedling or a cutting—the cuttings are fat at the bottom and the seedlings are thin at the base. Strong growers, ***Cereus peruvianus*** are often used as root stocks for grafting.

CEROPEGIA woodii

Ceropegia woodii (rosary vine, string of hearts, Chinese lantern plant) is a threadlike vine with opposite, heart-shaped, silver marked leaves. The flowers look like tiny purplish lanterns or baskets. The vines will grow very long and, since they tangle, some people prefer to keep them wrapped around a hoop. Give it filtered to bright light, organic soil with excellent drainage and very little water during its resting period. This is a plant that is not upset if it is not watered for a long time. The stems may all drop off, but new shoots will usually reappear when watering is restarted. Drench and let dry. It likes good dry air circulation and cool night temperatures. "Rosary vine" comes from the storage beads along the stem that help the plant through periods of neglect.

Crassula argentea

Crassula cornuta

CRASSULA

The ***Crassula*** are members of the crassula family. The family includes many succulent plants that adjust well to growing indoors. The care for aeoniums, crassulas, kalanchoes, sedums, etc., is about the same; they can be grown together easily. ***Crassula argentea*** (jade plant, Chinese rubber tree) is sometimes called ***Crassula arborescens*** by growers. The glossy, jade-green leaves are thick and fleshy and turn slightly red at the tips in the sun. The tips of the leaves are padded and the bottoms are flat. In time, the plant will grow into a many branched, thick stemmed, treelike succulent. The flowers are a very light pink. Even when young the jade plant's heavy stems give it the appearance of age. It can be trained into a bonsai shape for an elegant look or it can be planted in a mug. ***Crassula arborescens*** (silver dollar) is a treelike succulent with thick, grey stems. The flat grey-green leaves are fleshy and dotted with red. The flowers are white initially and gradually turn pink with age. ***Crassula cornuta*** has silvery-grey leaves that fit tightly together hiding the stem and making a distinctive column. ***Crassula 'Morgan's Pride'*** has compact clusters of large, flat, fleshy leaves. ***Crassula phyeurus*** has small, bright green leaves loosely growing on weak stems. It grows quickly and does especially well in a hanging pot. ***Crassula pyramidalis*** is a succulent with small, equal-sized, triangular, bright green leaves that are stacked on top of each other.

Crassulas prefer bright light but will tolerate less. Give them heavy soil with good drainage (some

Crassula argentea

Crassula 'Morgan's Pride'

Crassula phyeurus

Crassula 'Blue Jay'

pieces of broken up brick in the bottom of the pot help), cool night temperatures and good air circulation. Drench and let dry. Even if you wait until there is a slight shriveling of the leaves before watering, they will come right back. Overwatering and sitting in water can cause root rot. Underwatering is less dangerous than overwatering. Crassulas reproduce very easily from leaf and stem cuttings. Roots form more successfully if the cuttings are allowed to dry a week or more before being potted up. To make a leaf cutting, select a plump, healthy, mature leaf. Remove it from the stem with a gentle sideways pull. Place it somewhere that is warm and dry until the roots start to appear. Then pot it up.

ECHEVERIA

The ***Echeveria*** are rosette forming succulent plants with foliage that comes in a variety of shapes and colors. The flowers appear on the top of stalks that grow from between the leaves. The plant does not die after it has bloomed as do plants that have flowers which develop from the center growing point. Echeverias are natives of Mexico, Central and South America. Echeverias need bright light, heavy soil and excellent drainage. When grown in soilless mixes, they grow large and lush and lose their color and character. Many of the plants have a waxy sheen on their leaves. When they are watered over the top, the water collects in drops and spots the leaves when it dries. These spots are especially noticeable when the water is high in minerals. Drench and let dry. Water from below.

Echeveria species

Echeverias come from higher altitudes so give them dry air, cool night temperatures and good air circulation. As with other members of the crassula family (crassulas, kalanchoes, sedums, sempervivums, etc.), they reproduce easily from leaf cuttings.

Atanasio Echéverria, the Mexican botanical artist, drew thousands of illustrations of Mexican plants collected by Martin Sesse and Jose Mocino in the last years of the eighteenth century. The original drawings are now lost, but in 1820, the botanist Alphonse De Candolle was so impressed with them that he hired 120 draftsmen to work ten days straight to make tracings. In 1837, De Candolle honored Echeverria by naming the ***Echeveria*** after him.

Echinocactus grusonii

ECHINOCACTUS grusonii

Echinocactus grusonii (golden ball cactus, golden barrel cactus, hedgehog cactus, mother in law's chair) can grow into large globular plants over three feet in diameter. Slightly flattened on top, the globe is made up of twenty or more ribs. These ribs are covered with strong, arching, yellow spines which tend to fade to a dirty white or a grimy cream when the plants grow older. The yellow flowers bloom out of the creamy-white, wooly fuzz at the top of the plant. The fruit is covered with white wool. The seeds germinate quite readily. Care should be taken when transplanting the young plants since their roots are brittle and can break off easily. The seedlings can grow to be about four inches across in four years (see picture on page 15).

Give them bright light, heavy soil with excellent drainage (old broken bricks help) and cold to cool night temperatures. If echinocactus are not introduced gradually to full sun, they will sunburn and scar. The flesh is edible; in Mexico, it is sometimes candied. It can be a source of water in the desert.

EULYCHNIA saint-pieana

Eulychnia saint-pieana is a tall columnar cactus from the dry hills of Chile. It has many ribs which are set with large, white, wooly tufts accented by long central spines. The flowers stay open day and night. The fleshy fruit is edible, but not very tasty. Give it bright light, heavy soil, excellent drainage, cool nights and good air circulation.

Eulychnia saint-pieana

Euphorbia canariensis

Euphorbia grandicornis

EUPHORBIA

Euphorbia is the name given to a large group of over two thousand different plants which grow all over the world. The euphorbia that grow in cold climates are called spurges. Those that come from tropical and subtropical areas of the world take on many different appearances. Some from arid regions are very squat, plump and have sharp thorns. When not in bloom, it is very hard to tell them from cacti unless you stab them; the euphorbias have a milky sap. ***Euphorbia canariensis*** has four- to six-angled stems that have short twin spines growing along the crests. Some people find the sap quite irritating. ***Euphorbia candelabrum*** has four angled branches and has the appearance, if you use your imagination, of a giant candlestick. Where it grows outdoors, it is often used as a living fence. ***Euphorbia gatbergensis*** is a decrepit-looking, squat succulent. The fat stem is topped with a number of short branches. It is a plant that will give very little trouble and will always make you feel needed. ***Euphorbia grandicornis*** (cow's horn euphorbia) is a bright, pale green, spiny succulent. The spines are one to two inches long. From time to time it will have very small, ovalish leaves. ***Euphorbia horrida*** looks like a barrel cactus; its spines often occur in groups of three. It is very difficult to tell the male from the female plants until they flower. ***Euphorbia lactea*** has three- or four-angled dark green stems that usually are less than three inches in diameter and have creamy-white chevronlike markings. ***Euphorbia trigona*** is similar but much larger. ***Euphorbia mammillaris*** (corn cob

Euphorbia gatbergensis

cactus) looks like a green corn cob with spines. The spines, which are a half inch to an inch long, make it look a lot like a cactus—especially when the narrow, small leaves are not present. ***Euphorbia obesa*** is a flat, ball-shaped plant that comes in separate sexes that are difficult to tell apart unless you have a pair together. ***Euphorbia pulcherrima*** (poinsettia, Mexican flame flower) is a branching shrub that could grow twelve feet tall before hybridizing. Formerly thought of only as a Christmas plant, it is now being grown all year long. The poinsettia will sometimes lose all its leaves and go dormant after flowering. The plant is not poisonous despite many stories to the contrary. ***Euphorbia splendens*** (crown of thorns) is a shrub with grey stems, one half to one inch thick, covered with tough, inch-long spines. It has oval, bright green leaves and clusters of flowers that are set off by creamy-orange or bright red bracts. It will sometimes drop all of its leaves unexpectedly, which usually means that it is ready to take a rest. Hold off the water until the leaves start reappearing. This should occur in a month or so.

Euphorbia horrida

Euphorbia tirucalli

Euphorbia splendens

Euphorbia stenoclada, a beautiful but vicious plant, has sharp thorns on its silvery-grey stems. It spends most of its life out of leaf. ***Euphorbia tirucalli*** (milk bush, pencil cactus) is a small tree with pencil-thin, dark green, cylindrical branches. Its narrow leaves often fall off soon after appearing if the humidity is low. Some people are allergic to the milky sap.

The euphorbias prefer bright light, heavy soil with excellent drainage, circulating air and cool or house temperatures. When in bloom, the poinsettia should be kept evenly moist; otherwise, most euphorbias prefer to be drenched and let dry. Euphorbias are great indoor plants since they take well to dry air and are more tolerant of heat than cacti. When propagating from cuttings, let them dry a week before potting.

Euphorbia species. Euphorbia obesa in front, female (left), male (right)

Ferocactus

Gasteria

FEROCACTUS

The ***Ferocactus*** (ferocious cactus) get their name from their long, heavy, often hooked spines. These barrel-shaped cacti with prominent ribs used to be classed with the ***Echinocactus*** (barrel cactus) group. ***Ferocactus latispinus*** (devil's tongue cactus) gets its name from its long, broad, red-colored spines. Another with a flattened, red, central spine is ***Ferocactus recurvus*** (devil's pincushion). These cacti are easy to grow and can get quite large eventually. They like bright light, heavy soil with excellent drainage, house temperatures and good air circulation. In Mexico, the skin and spines are peeled off and the flesh is diced to be eaten raw or candied. They also provide an emergency source of water in the desert—you slice off the top of the plant, stir the pulp with a stick and drink the sap.

GASTERIA

The ***Gasteria*** get their name —which means stomach in Greek ('gaster')—from the shape of their flowers. They are plants with thick, succulent, tongue-shaped leaves that are arranged in stacks or spirals. They are very similar to the aloes except that their leaves are flatter and they have smooth edges. ***Gasteria verrucosa*** (ox tongue gasteria) has dark green leaves covered with white warts. Give them filtered to bright light, heavy soil with good drainage, cool night temperatures and dry circulating air. The tubelike flowers appear on the top of tall stems after a cold, dry rest period.

GYMNOCALYCIUM denudatum

Gymnocalycium denudatum (spider cactus), from southern Brazil, is a fat, globular cactus that gets its common name from the arrangement of its spines. It has very broad ribs and a slight "chin" beneath the yellowish spines. In very bright light this cactus takes on a brownish cast. A tiny cousin, ***Gymnocalycium mihanovichii***, has a bright red parasitic form called ***'Hibotan'*** that cannot survive unless it is grafted onto a cactus that provides chlorophyll and produces food for both. Give gymnocalycium bright light, heavy soil with excellent drainage, house temperatures and good air circulation. The many varieties grow easily from seed.

HAAGEOCEREUS chrysacranthus

Haageocereus chrysacranthus is a columnar cactus with many ribs and fine needlelike spines. Previously classified with the ***Cereus***, this cactus from Peru is one of those that can change its appearance with a less austere environment in the home of a loving collector. Plenty of food and drink, if it does not kill the plant with indigestion, will produce a fatter looking cactus with more ribs. Give it bright light, heavy soil with excellent drainage, cool to house temperatures and good air circulation. Since it is rather slow growing on its own roots, it is sometimes grafted on the roots of a more vigorous cousin.

Gymnocalycium denudatum

Haageocereus chrysacranthus

Hoya carnosa 'Variegata'

Hoya 'Krinkle'

HOYA

Hoyas (wax plants) are twining plants that belong to the milkweed family. They have thick, evergreen, waxy leaves. Their flowers look like a cluster of small pink and white stars and are fragrant and long lasting with a sweet nectar. The flowers grow out of little stubs which should not be removed when the plants have finished flowering since the stubs will usually flower again. ***Hoya bella*** is not as large-leaved or as vigorous as ***Hoya carnosa***, but when grown indoors, it will usually bloom quicker and more often. ***Hoya carnosa*** has green leaves that are sometimes spotted with white specks. Its variegated form, ***Hoya carnosa 'Variegata'***, has dark green leaves that are marked with cream and pink. ***Hoya imperialis*** is a tall climber with downy stems. It has large, leathery, dark green leaves and dull, purple, milkweedlike flowers. Hoyas need bright light, heavy soil, cool night temperatures and good air circulation. They can go a long time without water, but their growth slows down and their leaves start to shrivel. Their leaves drop after shriveling; if you let them go that long without water, they do not always come back. Hoyas seem to attract mealybugs, but these can be controlled by regular showers. Hoyas make attractive hanging baskets with their shiny leaves hanging down over the sides—or they can be trained up on a hoop. Whichever you decide, do it, and let them alone. They bloom better when they feel cozy in their pots.

KALANCHOE

Kalanchoes of Madagascar are easy growing indoor plants. ***Kalanchoe blossfeldiana*** is a compact plant with shiny, succulent, dark green leaves. It has clusters of red-orange flowers that appear in winter or whenever there are short days. Because of its sturdiness, it is often used as a holiday gift plant. ***Kalanchoe daigremontiana*** (air plant), which is sometimes known as ***Bryophyllum daigremontianum,*** is an erect plant with fleshy, brown-spotted, three-cornered leaves. Small plantlets often appear on the margins of the saw-toothed leaves. These plantlets can be potted up when they fall off or they can be left in the pot until they take hold on their own. ***Kalanchoe orgyalis*** is a slow growing plant that has oval, bronze-haired leaves two to two and a half inches long that turn grey as they grow older. ***Kalanchoe tomentosa*** (panda plant, pussy ears) is a succulent plant with erect, branching stems and fleshy, almond-shaped leaves. The leaves are covered with white furry felt and are marked with brown on the tips. Kalanchoes like bright light, heavy soil with good drainage, cool night temperatures and good air circulation. Drench and let dry. These plants can survive with very little water and almost freezing temperatures.

Kalanchoe tomentosa

Kalanchoe orgyalis

Lithops

LITHOPS

Lithops (living stones, pebble plants) are small succulent plants that look like little, weathered pebbles or split rocks. They have no stems and often will grow with only the tops showing. Seedlings sometimes seem to burrow into the ground. They can produce roots very quickly to take advantage of soil moisture. The roots dry up just as rapidly when the need for them is done. Lithops have large yellow or white daisylike flowers. Give them bright light, heavy sandy soil with excellent drainage, cool nights and good air circulation. Drench and let dry. Lithops usually like to rest from December through March. Watering during this time is a sure way to encourage root rot unless they seem extremely dry.

MAMMILLARIA

The ***Mammillaria*** (pincushion cacti) get their name from the Latin "*mammilla*; nipple". They are characterized chiefly by the nipple-shaped growths on their surfaces. Mammillarias are squat, dumpy, spherical or cylindrical

Mammillaria compressa

plants with no-fooling spines. Favorites with collectors because they grow easily and come in a variety of forms, they ask only a scant space for their homes. When in bloom, a garland of flowers forms around the top of the plant. Thin, red, colorful fruits appear and are often still on the plant until the flowers arrive the next season. ***Mammillaria compressa***, often known as ***Mammillaria angularis***, is globular and somewhat flattened on top. It is pale greyish-green and is covered with tufts of white wool and long white bristles. It is a tough plant that will grow in partial shade.

Mammillaria geminispina, sometimes known as ***Mammillaria bicolor*** or ***Mammillaria nobilis***, is a beautiful cactus that grows in clumps of bluish-green balls covered with tufts of white wool and white spines. This is an unusual cactus since it has a milky sap.

Give mammillarias bright light, heavy soil with excellent drainage (ground up rocks with a little soil), dry air, cool nights and good air circulation. Drench and let dry. While mammillaria seeds are slow to germinate and the seedlings are very slow growers, they grow into splendid plants. Since the mature

Mammillaria geminispina

Melocactus matanzanus

Nananthus schoonesii

plants also grow slowly, they do not require a bigger space for quite sometime. They continue to insure their welcome by flowering well.

MELOCACTUS matanzanus

Melocactus matanzanus (Turk's head cactus, Turk's cap cactus, melon cactus), from Mexico, is a large ribbed, ball-shaped or cylindrical plant that develops a cap or "cephalium" on the top of the plant at maturity. The cap in ***Melocactus matanzanus*** is white with red-orange bristles. The flowers, when they appear in the top, are a rosy-pink. ***Melocactus communis,*** from Jamaica, which has a similar appearance, was one of the first cacti ever seen by Europeans; they thought that the plants were actually the fruit of a giant thistle. These plants originate from warm, moist, coastal areas; unlike most desert cacti, they can tolerate humidity. Give them bright light, heavy soil with good drainage and warm nights. Drench and let dry.

NANANTHUS schoonesii

Nananthus schoonesii is a small, South African succulent that belongs to the same family as the ***Lithops*** and the ***Trichodiadema***. It has a compact, tuberous root system and opposite leaves. The single, daisylike flowers open after noon and close again when it becomes dark. The name nananthus means dwarf flower, but the flower is actually large when compared with the rest of the plant. Give nananthus bright light and heavy sandy soil with excellent drainage. It prefers cool nights and good air circulation.

Notocactus leninghausii on graft

Notocactus on its own roots

NOTOCACTUS leninghausii

Notocactus leninghausii (golden ball cactus, ball cactus) is a spherical to cylindrical cactus with many slightly warty ribs covered with long, hairlike, golden spines. It can grow three feet tall and flowers only when it is tall enough. The large, yellow flowers grow out of the middle of the white wool which covers the top. When they are large enough to flower, sprouts often start growing up around the bottom of the main stem. Give them bright light, heavy soil with excellent drainage, cold night temperatures and good air circulation. Drench and let dry, but watch the watering. Since the roots rot easily, it is often grafted onto a more tolerant root stock.

OPUNTIA

Opuntia (prickly pears, bunny ears, beaver tails) can grow indoors or outdoors from Alaska to the tip of South America. Single species can vary greatly under different soils and climates. Some can be found growing in areas of heavy rainfall; others can winter happily outside in the Lake Michigan sand dunes. Their total height can vary from a few inches to twenty feet. Opuntias usually have jointed cylindrical or pancake-shaped pads. They often have large spines

Opuntia microdasys

which are less bothersome than the glochides (tufts of fishhook prickles) that break off and stick in the fingers. Edible fruits follow beautiful flowers in several opuntias. These fruits are cultivated as a food crop in several parts of the world. Sometimes new joints or new fruit can develop from the old fruit. Since these cacti are enthusiastic growers outdoors, they can become weeds if not kept under control. ***Opuntia microdasys*** (bunny ears) gets its name from its flat elongated pads that look like rabbit ears. It comes in a number of forms which are easy to identify because the pads are covered with a neat pattern of large tufts of glochides with hardly any spines.

Opuntias generally like bright light, heavy soil, cool to house temperatures and good air circulation. Drench and let dry.

Opuntia species

Oreocereus hendriksenianus

OREOCEREUS hendriksenianus densilanatus

Oreocereus hendriksenianus densilanatus (mountain cereus) is a strongly ribbed cactus from the Andes of Bolivia and Peru. It has reddish spines and long, silky hair that can get rather dirty from dust and pollution. Give it bright light and well drained, heavy soil. Keep it cool and dry during the winter. Whenever it looks like a dirty old man, gently shampoo its hair and brush it out with a soft toothbrush.

PORTULACARIA afra

Portulacaria afra (elephant bush) is a succulent bush with thick grey or brownish stems and fat, juicy, bright green leaves. It has the appearance of a sparse, small-leafed jade plant. Elephants eat it; it can get six feet tall indoors if you do not have many elephants around. Give it bright light, heavy soil with excellent drainage, cool night temperatures and good air circulation. Drench and let dry—it will tolerate almost everything except overwatering. If you underwater, the leaves will shrivel but will plump up again if you water before they drop off the plant. There are also varieties with mottled or variegated leaves—some yellow, some pink and some with very small green leaves. The small-leafed and variegated varieties are slower growing and appreciate having more attention. They can be pruned to a decorative bonsai style with the appearance of great age.

Portulacaria afra

Rebutia

REBUTIA

The ***Rebutia*** are small ball or barrel-shaped cacti with small spines that look a lot like the ***Mammillaria,*** but their tubercles are arranged in spirals. The flowers come in a variety of colors and are sometimes larger than the plant. Rebutias are among the better indoor bloomers. Their flowers, which close up at night, will last four or five days. Rebutias need bright light, heavy soil with excellent drainage, good air circulation and cool to cold night temperatures. They prefer to be drenched and let dry.

Sansevieria assortment

SANSEVIERIA

The ***Sansevierias*** (bow-string hemp, mother in law's tongue) are plants with stiff, erect, leathery leaves that are flat in some species and cylindrical in others. ***Sansevieria cylindrica*** has leaves that are round in a cross section like an animal's horn. Although a slow grower, it is a fascinating plant to have in a collection of succulents —once seen, you will never forget its shape. ***Sansevieria trifasciata 'Laurentii'*** (yellow banded mother in law's tongue) are erect plants with flat, thick, leathery, dark green leaves with lighter green cross markings. Well grown plants will get over five feet tall indoors and will often bloom with a cloudlike bunch of fragrant white flowers. ***Sansevieria trifasciata 'Hahnii'*** (birdnest sansevieria) has a full rosette of short wide leaves. In addition to the common dark green form there are also yellow banded

Schlumbergera

(gold) and pale green (silver) variations. Although sansevierias prefer bright light, they will take almost any light they can get. They prefer to be drenched and let dry between waterings, dry air and house temperatures, heavy soil and good drainage. Very tolerant plants, they will take almost any condition except overwatering.

SCHLUMBERGERA species and hybrids

The ***Schlumbergera*** (holiday cacti) get their common names from their time of flowering: Thanksgiving, Christmas, Easter, etc. Their scientific names are in an interesting state because of the hybridization that has taken place over the years. They come from the jungles of tropical South America and are similar, but smaller, than the ***Epiphyllum*** (orchid cacti). Most of them are epiphytic (grow high in trees) and have no spines. They have flat, jointed leaves that grow in chains one to two feet long. The flowers range in color from white through rose, red, lavender and purple. They need short days (eight hours) or cold nights (55°F) for flowering. Give schlumbergera filtered to bright light and organic soil with good drainage. Keep the plants evenly moist while they are actively growing, and drench and let dry during their resting period. If the soil gets too dry, the end joints drop off; if it gets too wet, the plant will rot.

Sedum

SEDUM

The ***Sedum*** come primarily from the northern hemisphere. The name sedum comes from the Latin "*sedeo*; I sit," which suggests that many of them will sit and grow anywhere they happen to land. The hardy sedums are ideal rock garden plants since they will grow for years in spots that other plants find inhospitable. ***Sedum acre*** (stonecrop) is a creeping plant with thin stems covered with small, yellow-green succulent leaves. The cheerful yellow flowers look like small stars. Hardy outdoors, it is an attractive plant indoors. It is especially handy to have if, like Pliny, you believe that wrapping a section in black cloth and slipping it under your pillow will cure insomnia. ***Sedum morganianum*** (burro tail, donkey's tail) has weak, brittle stems that sometimes hang more than five feet below the pot. ***Sedum rubrotinctum*** (Christmas cheer), sometimes known as ***Sedum guatemalense***, has thick, fleshy, green leaves tipped with red. The brighter the light is, the redder the leaves become. ***Sedum lineare 'Variegatum'*** is a spreading, low growing succulent with small, narrow, pointed leaves that are edged with creamy-white. It does well in hanging baskets that are hard to water. ***Sedum sieboldii***, which is somewhat hardy outdoors, has stems that grow from thick roots like the spokes of a wheel. The leaves are round and have serrated edges which are often red. There is also a variegated form that is streaked with white.

Give sedums bright light, heavy soil with good drainage, cool night temperatures and good air circula-

Sedum morganianum

tion. Drench and let dry. The leaves will shrivel if they go without water for months, but the plant will revive if watered before all the leaves drop.

SEMPERVIVUM tectorum

Sempervivum tectorum (hens and chickens, roof-houseleek) grows in a flat, three to four inch rosette of grey-green leaves tipped with brown. Pink flowers appear on the top of a longish flower stalk. The Emperor Charlemagne ordered every roof to be planted with them as a protection against lightning. Since the rosettes die after blooming it was (and still is in some areas) considered unlucky to let them flower. They need bright light, heavy soil with good drainage, cold night temperatures and good air circulation. Drench ånd let dry. The plants will exist for a long time with very little moisture and can be used decoratively in wreaths of dried materials.

Sempervivum tectorum

Senecio assortment (from left to right): Senecio mikanioides, Senecio articulatus, Senecio scaposus, Senecio serpens

SENECIO

The ***Senecio*** are a large group of plants that belong to the daisy family. Most of the succulent species originate in South Africa. They come in a variety of shapes and colors. All can take 45°F temperatures in the winter, and some varieties will sulk if they are too warm. ***Senecio articulatus***, sometimes known as ***Kleinia articulata***, (cigar plant, candle plant) has stems formed from a series of connecting three to five inch joints or "cigars." Both the "cigars" and the ivy-shaped leaves are blue-grey. ***Senecio cruentus*** (cineraria of florists) has large, heart-shaped leaves and many beautiful white or bright colored flowers. They need plenty of water when they are in bloom. They are often heartbreakers indoors because they quickly go to pieces when night temperatures get above 50°F. ***Senecio macroglossus variegatus*** (variegated German ivy) has weak stems that will grow either upwards or downwards. The thick, waxy leaves are dark green with creamy-yellow variegation. The small, white flowers have yellow centers. ***Senecio mikanioides*** (German ivy, parlor ivy) stands up well in dry air and is a good substitute for English ivy. It has ivy-shaped, bright green leaves and small, fragrant yellow flowers. ***Senecio rowleyanus*** (string of pearls) originated in bright, sunny South Africa. The weak threadlike stems can hang down three feet. The beadlike leaves are especially adapted for water storage. The translucent, striped veins control the amount of light that gets into the center of the leaves. The flowers are small, fluffy, dirty-white brushes with purplish-brown spots.

Senecio macroglossus variegatus

Senecio rowleyanus

Stapelia

Senecio scaposus is an almost stemless plant. The two to three inch cylindrical leaves grow in a tight rosette. When young, the leaves are covered with a white felt; the leaves become a smooth green when they get older. Do not overwater it. ***Senecio serpens*** are much-branched plants with cylindrical leaves flattened on one side. The leaves are covered with a bluish sheen.

Some senecios need more water than others. Generally, give them bright light, heavy soil with excellent drainage, drench and let dry.

STAPELIA

The hundred or so species of ***Stapelia*** (carrion flower, starfish flower) are all quite short and branch up from their base. Until they flower they look a bit like cacti with grey-green, velvety stems six to eight inches long. Their star-shaped flowers (which sometimes smell like rotting meat) and the seeds, with the silky hairs attached, help identify stapelias as members of the milkweed family. Though they prefer bright light, they can sunburn in hot summer sun. They are shallow rooted and do not care to be crowded. The soil should have excellent drainage. Do not overwater —drench and then let dry between waterings. In the winter, water only enough to keep the plants from shriveling. They grow easily from seed; the shoots, cut off at the thinnest part, will root easily.

TEPHROCACTUS

The ***Tephrocactus*** from South America are very similar to the ***Opuntia*** and are often classed with them. Their thick, short joints are globular or cylindrical. When they are very young they have tiny leaves that soon disappear. They have many glochids (barbed hairs or bristles) that break off in the hand at the slightest touch and are found sometimes even inside the fruit. The spines are usually long and add interest to the plant. ***Tephrocactus flexispinus*** is made up of globular sections that are covered with flexible spines. ***Tephrocactus paediphylla*** has very long spines that are somewhat flattened and twisted. The spines grow out of cylindrical segments that grow on top of each other a bit like sausages. Give them bright light, heavy soil with excellent drainage (broken up bricks do very well) and drench and let dry. They are slow growers and do not need much water even in the summer time. In fact, with these, less is usually better than more. They will tolerate dry air and winter temperatures just above freezing.

Tephrocactus flexispinus

Tephrocactus paediphylla

Trichodiadema olearea

TRICHODIADEMA olearea

Trichodiadema olearea belongs to the same family as the ***Lithops.*** It is a shrubby succulent with long, slender, arched branches and short, plump, cylindrical leaves. At the end of each leaf is a cluster of small, hairy bristles or spines. This cluster, or crown, is responsible for its scientific name "*tricho*; hair;" "*diademea*; crown." At night, moisture condenses on these hairs and the water is collected down into the tip of the leaf. In seedlings these "hair crowns" appear very large in proportion to the leaf.

Give it bright light, cool nights, good air circulation and heavy soil with excellent drainage. Do not overwater. Drench and let dry.

Yucca elephantipes

YUCCA elephantipes

Yucca elephantipes (spineless yucca, palm lily) from Mexico and Guatemala looks a lot like a fat dracaena. Bought as yucca tips, the plant is a large rosette of sword shaped, grass-green leaves. With age the plant loses its lower leaves and develops a trunk which can get over forty feet tall when grown outside. Given strong light and plenty of encouragement, they can soon grow eight or nine feet high indoors. Yuccas prefer bright light and heavy soil with good drainage. Though they are not really succulents, they can go a long time between drinks. Give them a good long drink when you do water. Yuccas are tolerant of temperature but prefer cool nights and dry air.

Index

D

E

F

G

H

R

S

T

V

W

Y